50 Party Snacks Recipes

By: Kelly Johnson

Table of Contents

- Mini Caprese Skewers
- Spinach and Artichoke Dip
- Cheese and Charcuterie Board
- Guacamole and Chips
- Deviled Eggs
- Buffalo Chicken Wings
- Stuffed Mushrooms
- Bacon-Wrapped Dates
- Veggie Platter with Hummus
- Mozzarella Sticks
- Mini Meatballs
- Nachos Supreme
- Pigs in a Blanket
- Shrimp Cocktail
- Guacamole-Stuffed Mini Peppers
- Spinach and Cheese Puffs
- Sweet and Spicy Popcorn
- Mini Quesadillas
- Baked Brie with Jam
- Mini Tacos
- Loaded Potato Skins
- Hummus and Pita Chips
- Fried Pickles
- Parmesan Crisps
- Grilled Shrimp Skewers
- Stuffed Jalapeños
- Spinach and Feta Puffs
- Guacamole and Salsa Trio
- Chicken Tenders with Honey Mustard
- Veggie Spring Rolls
- Baked Zucchini Fries
- Mini Pizza Bites
- Antipasto Skewers
- Cheddar and Bacon Biscuits
- Sweet Potato Chips

- Roasted Chickpeas
- Cucumber Bites with Cream Cheese
- Caprese Salad Cups
- Caramelized Onion Dip
- Coconut Shrimp
- Veggie Fritters
- Taco Dip
- Chicken Sliders
- Roasted Garlic and Parmesan Popcorn
- Fruit and Cheese Skewers
- Nacho Bites
- Parmesan and Herb Crackers
- Stuffed Mini Croissants
- Sweet and Savory Chex Mix
- Meat and Cheese Sliders

Mini Caprese Skewers

Ingredients:

- 1 pint cherry tomatoes
- 1 package fresh mozzarella balls (bocconcini or ciliegine)
- Fresh basil leaves
- Balsamic glaze
- Salt and pepper to taste

Instructions:

1. Thread a cherry tomato, a basil leaf, and a mozzarella ball onto small skewers or toothpicks.
2. Arrange on a serving platter and drizzle with balsamic glaze.
3. Sprinkle with salt and pepper to taste. Serve immediately.

Spinach and Artichoke Dip

Ingredients:

- 1 can (14 oz) artichoke hearts, drained and chopped
- 1 cup frozen spinach, thawed and squeezed dry
- 1 cup cream cheese, softened
- 1/2 cup sour cream
- 1/2 cup mayonnaise
- 1 cup grated Parmesan cheese
- 1 cup shredded mozzarella cheese
- 1 clove garlic, minced
- Salt and pepper to taste

Instructions:

1. Preheat the oven to 375°F (190°C). In a bowl, mix cream cheese, sour cream, mayonnaise, Parmesan, mozzarella, garlic, spinach, and artichokes.
2. Season with salt and pepper, then transfer to a baking dish.
3. Bake for 20-25 minutes until bubbly and golden on top. Serve warm with crackers, bread, or veggies.

Cheese and Charcuterie Board

Ingredients:

- A variety of cheeses (brie, cheddar, goat cheese, blue cheese)
- Assorted cured meats (prosciutto, salami, chorizo)
- Crackers and baguette slices
- Fresh fruits (grapes, figs, apple slices)
- Nuts (almonds, walnuts)
- Olives and pickles
- Honey or fig jam (optional)

Instructions:

1. Arrange the cheeses, meats, and accompaniments on a large board or platter.
2. Add small bowls of olives, nuts, and jam. Fill the gaps with crackers, bread, and fresh fruit.
3. Serve immediately and enjoy.

Guacamole and Chips

Ingredients:

- 3 ripe avocados, peeled and pitted
- 1/2 small red onion, finely chopped
- 1 jalapeño, minced (optional)
- 1 lime, juiced
- 1/4 cup fresh cilantro, chopped
- Salt and pepper to taste
- Tortilla chips for serving

Instructions:

1. Mash the avocados in a bowl. Stir in onion, jalapeño, lime juice, cilantro, salt, and pepper.
2. Taste and adjust seasoning if necessary. Serve with tortilla chips.

Deviled Eggs

Ingredients:

- 6 hard-boiled eggs, peeled
- 1/4 cup mayonnaise
- 1 teaspoon mustard
- 1 teaspoon vinegar
- 1/4 teaspoon salt
- 1/8 teaspoon pepper
- Paprika for garnish

Instructions:

1. Cut the hard-boiled eggs in half and remove the yolks.
2. Mash the yolks with mayonnaise, mustard, vinegar, salt, and pepper.
3. Spoon or pipe the yolk mixture back into the egg whites.
4. Garnish with a sprinkle of paprika and serve chilled.

Buffalo Chicken Wings

Ingredients:

- 10 chicken wings
- 1/2 cup hot sauce
- 2 tablespoons butter, melted
- 1 teaspoon garlic powder
- Salt and pepper to taste
- Blue cheese or ranch dressing for dipping (optional)

Instructions:

1. Preheat the oven to 400°F (200°C). Place wings on a baking sheet and season with salt and pepper.
2. Bake for 20-25 minutes until crispy and cooked through.
3. In a bowl, combine hot sauce, melted butter, and garlic powder.
4. Toss the cooked wings in the buffalo sauce. Serve with dipping sauce if desired.

Stuffed Mushrooms

Ingredients:

- 12 large mushrooms, stems removed
- 4 oz cream cheese, softened
- 1/4 cup grated Parmesan cheese
- 1/4 cup breadcrumbs
- 1 tablespoon fresh parsley, chopped
- 1 clove garlic, minced
- Salt and pepper to taste

Instructions:

1. Preheat the oven to 375°F (190°C). Place the mushroom caps on a baking sheet.
2. In a bowl, combine cream cheese, Parmesan, breadcrumbs, parsley, garlic, salt, and pepper.
3. Stuff the mushroom caps with the cheese mixture and bake for 15-20 minutes until golden and bubbly.

Bacon-Wrapped Dates

Ingredients:

- 12 Medjool dates, pitted
- 6 slices bacon, cut in half
- Toothpicks for securing

Instructions:

1. Preheat the oven to 375°F (190°C). Wrap each date with a half slice of bacon and secure with a toothpick.
2. Place the bacon-wrapped dates on a baking sheet.
3. Bake for 12-15 minutes, turning occasionally, until the bacon is crispy.
4. Serve warm.

Veggie Platter with Hummus

Ingredients:

- Assorted fresh vegetables (carrot sticks, celery, cucumber slices, cherry tomatoes, bell pepper strips)
- 1 cup hummus (store-bought or homemade)

Instructions:

1. Arrange the fresh vegetables on a large platter.
2. Serve with a bowl of hummus in the center for dipping.

Mozzarella Sticks

Ingredients:

- 12 mozzarella sticks
- 1/2 cup flour
- 2 eggs, beaten
- 1 cup breadcrumbs
- 1/2 teaspoon garlic powder
- 1/4 teaspoon paprika
- Vegetable oil for frying
- Marinara sauce for dipping

Instructions:

1. Freeze mozzarella sticks for at least 30 minutes to prevent melting during frying.
2. Dredge each stick in flour, dip in egg, and coat in breadcrumbs mixed with garlic powder and paprika.
3. Heat oil in a pan over medium-high heat and fry the mozzarella sticks for 2-3 minutes until golden brown.
4. Drain on paper towels and serve with marinara sauce.

Mini Meatballs

Ingredients:

- 1 lb ground beef
- 1/2 cup breadcrumbs
- 1/4 cup grated Parmesan cheese
- 1 egg
- 1 teaspoon garlic powder
- Salt and pepper to taste
- 1/2 cup marinara sauce

Instructions:

1. Preheat the oven to 375°F (190°C). In a bowl, mix ground beef, breadcrumbs, Parmesan, egg, garlic powder, salt, and pepper.
2. Form the mixture into small meatballs and place on a baking sheet.
3. Bake for 12-15 minutes until cooked through.
4. Heat marinara sauce in a pan and toss meatballs in the sauce before serving.

Nachos Supreme

Ingredients:

- 1 bag tortilla chips
- 1 cup cooked ground beef or shredded chicken
- 1 cup shredded cheddar cheese
- 1 cup shredded Monterey Jack cheese
- 1/2 cup sour cream
- 1/4 cup salsa
- 1/4 cup jalapeños, sliced
- 1/4 cup green onions, chopped
- 1/4 cup black olives, sliced (optional)

Instructions:

1. Preheat the oven to 375°F (190°C). Spread tortilla chips evenly on a baking sheet.
2. Top with cooked ground beef or chicken, then sprinkle with shredded cheddar and Monterey Jack cheese.
3. Bake for 10-12 minutes until cheese is melted.
4. Top with sour cream, salsa, jalapeños, green onions, and black olives (if using). Serve immediately.

Pigs in a Blanket

Ingredients:

- 1 package mini cocktail sausages
- 1 can refrigerated crescent roll dough
- 1 tablespoon mustard (optional)

Instructions:

1. Preheat the oven to 375°F (190°C). Unroll the crescent roll dough and cut it into small triangles.
2. Place a mini sausage at the wide end of each dough triangle and roll it up.
3. Arrange the rolls on a baking sheet and bake for 10-12 minutes until golden brown.
4. Serve with mustard or ketchup for dipping.

Shrimp Cocktail

Ingredients:

- 1 lb cooked shrimp, peeled and deveined
- 1/2 cup cocktail sauce
- 1 tablespoon fresh lemon juice
- Lemon wedges for garnish

Instructions:

1. Arrange the cooked shrimp on a platter.
2. In a small bowl, mix cocktail sauce with fresh lemon juice.
3. Serve shrimp with cocktail sauce and lemon wedges on the side.

Guacamole-Stuffed Mini Peppers

Ingredients:

- 12 mini bell peppers, halved and seeded
- 1 ripe avocado, mashed
- 1 tablespoon lime juice
- 1 tablespoon cilantro, chopped
- 1/4 teaspoon garlic powder
- Salt and pepper to taste

Instructions:

1. In a bowl, combine mashed avocado, lime juice, cilantro, garlic powder, salt, and pepper.
2. Stuff each mini bell pepper half with the guacamole mixture.
3. Serve immediately as a fresh and colorful appetizer.

Spinach and Cheese Puffs

Ingredients:

- 1 sheet puff pastry, thawed
- 1/2 cup cooked spinach, drained and chopped
- 1/2 cup ricotta cheese
- 1/4 cup mozzarella cheese, shredded
- 1 egg, beaten
- Salt and pepper to taste

Instructions:

1. Preheat the oven to 375°F (190°C). Roll out the puff pastry and cut it into squares.
2. In a bowl, mix cooked spinach, ricotta, mozzarella, salt, and pepper.
3. Place a spoonful of the spinach mixture in the center of each puff pastry square and fold over to form a pocket.
4. Brush with the beaten egg and bake for 15-20 minutes until golden brown.

Sweet and Spicy Popcorn

Ingredients:

- 1/2 cup popcorn kernels (or 1 bag microwave popcorn)
- 2 tablespoons butter, melted
- 1 tablespoon honey
- 1/2 teaspoon cayenne pepper
- Salt to taste

Instructions:

1. Pop the popcorn according to package instructions or on the stove.
2. In a bowl, mix melted butter, honey, cayenne pepper, and salt.
3. Drizzle the sweet and spicy mixture over the popcorn and toss to coat. Serve immediately.

Mini Quesadillas

Ingredients:

- 4 small flour tortillas
- 1 cup shredded cheese (cheddar, mozzarella, or a blend)
- 1/2 cup cooked chicken or beef (optional)
- 1 tablespoon olive oil
- Salsa for dipping

Instructions:

1. Heat a pan over medium heat and lightly brush one side of each tortilla with olive oil.
2. Place one tortilla in the pan and sprinkle with cheese and any other toppings (chicken or beef). Top with another tortilla.
3. Cook until the bottom is golden, then flip and cook the other side until golden and crispy.
4. Remove from heat, slice into wedges, and serve with salsa.

Baked Brie with Jam

Ingredients:

- 1 wheel of Brie cheese
- 1/4 cup fruit jam (raspberry, apricot, or fig)
- 1 sheet puff pastry
- 1 egg, beaten (for egg wash)
- Crackers or baguette slices for serving

Instructions:

1. Preheat the oven to 375°F (190°C). Unroll the puff pastry and place the Brie in the center.
2. Spoon fruit jam over the top of the Brie. Fold the pastry over the cheese to cover it.
3. Brush the pastry with the beaten egg and bake for 20-25 minutes until golden brown.
4. Serve with crackers or baguette slices.

Mini Tacos

Ingredients:

- 12 mini taco shells or tortillas
- 1 cup cooked ground beef or shredded chicken
- 1/2 cup shredded cheese
- 1/4 cup lettuce, chopped
- 1/4 cup salsa
- Sour cream (optional)

Instructions:

1. Preheat the oven to 350°F (175°C). Arrange mini taco shells on a baking sheet.
2. Fill each taco shell with ground beef or chicken, then top with cheese.
3. Bake for 5-7 minutes until the cheese is melted.
4. Garnish with lettuce, salsa, and a dollop of sour cream. Serve immediately.

Loaded Potato Skins

Ingredients:

- 4 large russet potatoes
- 1 cup shredded cheddar cheese
- 1/4 cup sour cream
- 1/4 cup cooked bacon, crumbled
- 2 green onions, chopped
- Salt and pepper to taste

Instructions:

1. Preheat the oven to 400°F (200°C). Pierce the potatoes with a fork and bake for 45-50 minutes until tender.
2. Let the potatoes cool, then cut them in half and scoop out the flesh, leaving a border of potato.
3. Place the skins back on a baking sheet and bake for 10 minutes to crisp up.
4. Fill each skin with cheese and bacon, then bake for another 5-7 minutes until the cheese is melted.
5. Top with sour cream and green onions before serving.

Hummus and Pita Chips

Ingredients:

- 1 cup hummus (store-bought or homemade)
- 4 pita bread pockets
- Olive oil for brushing
- 1 teaspoon paprika (optional)

Instructions:

1. Preheat the oven to 375°F (190°C). Slice pita bread into triangles.
2. Arrange pita triangles on a baking sheet and brush with olive oil. Sprinkle with paprika if desired.
3. Bake for 10-12 minutes until crispy and golden.
4. Serve with hummus for dipping.

Fried Pickles

Ingredients:

- 1 jar dill pickle slices
- 1 cup all-purpose flour
- 1 teaspoon garlic powder
- 1 teaspoon paprika
- 1/2 teaspoon salt
- 1/4 teaspoon black pepper
- 1 egg, beaten
- 1 cup breadcrumbs
- Vegetable oil for frying
- Ranch or blue cheese dressing for dipping

Instructions:

1. Heat oil in a deep pan or fryer to 375°F (190°C).
2. In a bowl, mix flour, garlic powder, paprika, salt, and pepper.
3. Dip pickle slices first in the flour mixture, then in the beaten egg, and coat with breadcrumbs.
4. Fry the pickles in batches for 2-3 minutes until golden brown and crispy.
5. Drain on paper towels and serve with ranch or blue cheese dressing.

Parmesan Crisps

Ingredients:

- 1 cup grated Parmesan cheese
- 1/2 teaspoon garlic powder (optional)
- Fresh herbs for garnish (optional)

Instructions:

1. Preheat the oven to 400°F (200°C) and line a baking sheet with parchment paper.
2. Spoon small piles of Parmesan cheese onto the baking sheet, spreading them out into circles.
3. Sprinkle garlic powder and fresh herbs if using.
4. Bake for 3-5 minutes until the cheese is melted and crispy.
5. Let cool slightly before serving as a snack or topping for soups and salads.

Grilled Shrimp Skewers

Ingredients:

- 1 lb large shrimp, peeled and deveined
- 2 tablespoons olive oil
- 1 tablespoon lemon juice
- 2 garlic cloves, minced
- 1 tablespoon fresh parsley, chopped
- Salt and pepper to taste
- Wooden or metal skewers

Instructions:

1. Preheat the grill to medium-high heat.
2. In a bowl, combine olive oil, lemon juice, garlic, parsley, salt, and pepper.
3. Toss shrimp in the marinade and let sit for 15-20 minutes.
4. Thread shrimp onto skewers.
5. Grill shrimp for 2-3 minutes per side until pink and cooked through.
6. Serve immediately with a squeeze of lemon.

Stuffed Jalapeños

Ingredients:

- 12 fresh jalapeños, halved and seeded
- 8 oz cream cheese, softened
- 1/2 cup shredded cheddar cheese
- 1/4 teaspoon garlic powder
- 1/4 teaspoon smoked paprika
- 1/4 cup cooked bacon, crumbled (optional)

Instructions:

1. Preheat the oven to 375°F (190°C). Arrange jalapeño halves on a baking sheet.
2. In a bowl, mix cream cheese, cheddar cheese, garlic powder, paprika, and crumbled bacon.
3. Spoon the cheese mixture into the jalapeño halves.
4. Bake for 20-25 minutes until the peppers are tender and the cheese is bubbly.
5. Serve warm.

Spinach and Feta Puffs

Ingredients:

- 1 sheet puff pastry, thawed
- 1 cup cooked spinach, drained and chopped
- 1/2 cup crumbled feta cheese
- 1 tablespoon olive oil
- 1/4 teaspoon garlic powder
- 1 egg, beaten (for egg wash)

Instructions:

1. Preheat the oven to 375°F (190°C).
2. Roll out the puff pastry and cut it into squares.
3. In a bowl, combine spinach, feta, olive oil, and garlic powder.
4. Place a spoonful of the spinach mixture in the center of each pastry square.
5. Fold the pastry over the filling and seal the edges. Brush with beaten egg.
6. Bake for 15-20 minutes until golden and puffed.

Guacamole and Salsa Trio

For Guacamole:

- 2 ripe avocados, mashed
- 1 small tomato, chopped
- 1/4 onion, finely chopped
- 1 tablespoon lime juice
- 1 tablespoon cilantro, chopped
- Salt and pepper to taste

For Salsa Verde:

- 1 cup tomatillos, husked and roasted
- 1/4 cup cilantro, chopped
- 1 tablespoon lime juice
- Salt to taste

For Classic Salsa:

- 1 cup fresh tomatoes, chopped
- 1/4 onion, finely chopped
- 1 tablespoon cilantro, chopped
- 1 jalapeño, finely chopped (optional)
- Salt and pepper to taste

Instructions:

1. For guacamole, combine mashed avocados, tomato, onion, lime juice, cilantro, salt, and pepper in a bowl. Mix well.
2. For salsa verde, blend roasted tomatillos, cilantro, lime juice, and salt in a blender until smooth.
3. For classic salsa, mix chopped tomatoes, onion, cilantro, jalapeño, salt, and pepper in a bowl.
4. Serve all three with tortilla chips.

Chicken Tenders with Honey Mustard

Ingredients:

- 1 lb chicken tenders
- 1 cup breadcrumbs
- 1/2 cup flour
- 1 egg, beaten
- Salt and pepper to taste
- Vegetable oil for frying

For Honey Mustard Sauce:

- 1/4 cup honey
- 1/4 cup mustard
- 1 tablespoon mayonnaise
- 1 tablespoon lemon juice

Instructions:

1. Preheat the oil in a pan over medium heat. Season chicken tenders with salt and pepper.
2. Coat each chicken tender in flour, then dip into beaten egg, and coat with breadcrumbs.
3. Fry the chicken tenders for 4-5 minutes per side until golden and crispy.
4. For the sauce, whisk together honey, mustard, mayonnaise, and lemon juice.
5. Serve chicken tenders with the honey mustard sauce for dipping.

Veggie Spring Rolls

Ingredients:

- 10 rice paper wrappers
- 1/2 cup shredded carrots
- 1/2 cup cucumber, julienned
- 1/4 cup fresh cilantro
- 1/4 cup fresh mint leaves
- 1/4 cup bell pepper, thinly sliced
- 1/4 cup vermicelli noodles, cooked
- 1/4 cup soy sauce (for dipping)

Instructions:

1. Soak rice paper wrappers in warm water for 10-15 seconds until soft.
2. Lay each wrapper flat and layer with carrots, cucumber, cilantro, mint, bell pepper, and noodles.
3. Roll up tightly and cut in half. Serve with soy sauce for dipping.

Baked Zucchini Fries

Ingredients:

- 2 medium zucchinis, cut into fries
- 1/2 cup breadcrumbs
- 1/4 cup grated Parmesan cheese
- 1 teaspoon garlic powder
- 1 teaspoon dried oregano
- Salt and pepper to taste
- 1 egg, beaten
- Olive oil spray

Instructions:

1. Preheat the oven to 400°F (200°C) and line a baking sheet with parchment paper.
2. In a bowl, mix breadcrumbs, Parmesan, garlic powder, oregano, salt, and pepper.
3. Dip each zucchini fry into the beaten egg, then coat in the breadcrumb mixture.
4. Arrange the fries on the baking sheet and lightly spray with olive oil.
5. Bake for 20-25 minutes until crispy and golden.

Mini Pizza Bites

Ingredients:

- 1 package pizza dough (or homemade dough)
- 1/2 cup marinara sauce
- 1 cup shredded mozzarella cheese
- 1/4 cup pepperoni slices, chopped
- 1/4 cup bell pepper, chopped
- 1 tablespoon olive oil

Instructions:

1. Preheat the oven to 375°F (190°C). Roll out the pizza dough and cut into small circles.
2. Place each dough circle on a greased baking sheet. Top with a spoonful of marinara sauce, cheese, pepperoni, and bell pepper.
3. Bake for 8-10 minutes until the cheese is melted and the dough is golden.
4. Serve warm.

Antipasto Skewers

Ingredients:

- 12 small wooden skewers
- 12 cherry tomatoes
- 12 cubes mozzarella cheese
- 12 slices salami or pepperoni
- 12 kalamata olives
- 12 small pickles (optional)
- Fresh basil leaves (optional)
- Balsamic glaze (optional)

Instructions:

1. Thread cherry tomatoes, mozzarella, salami, olives, and pickles onto the skewers.
2. If desired, add a fresh basil leaf to each skewer.
3. Drizzle with balsamic glaze before serving (optional). Serve immediately.

Cheddar and Bacon Biscuits

Ingredients:

- 2 cups all-purpose flour
- 1 tablespoon baking powder
- 1/2 teaspoon salt
- 1/2 teaspoon garlic powder
- 1/2 cup cold butter, cubed
- 1 cup shredded sharp cheddar cheese
- 1/4 cup cooked bacon, crumbled
- 3/4 cup milk

Instructions:

1. Preheat the oven to 400°F (200°C). In a bowl, mix flour, baking powder, salt, and garlic powder.
2. Cut in the cold butter until the mixture resembles coarse crumbs.
3. Stir in cheddar cheese, crumbled bacon, and milk until just combined.
4. Drop spoonfuls of dough onto a greased baking sheet.
5. Bake for 10-12 minutes until golden brown. Serve warm.

Sweet Potato Chips

Ingredients:

- 2 large sweet potatoes, thinly sliced
- 2 tablespoons olive oil
- 1 teaspoon paprika
- 1/2 teaspoon garlic powder
- Salt to taste

Instructions:

1. Preheat the oven to 400°F (200°C) and line a baking sheet with parchment paper.
2. Toss sweet potato slices with olive oil, paprika, garlic powder, and salt.
3. Spread the slices in a single layer on the baking sheet.
4. Bake for 20-25 minutes, flipping halfway through, until crispy and golden. Let cool before serving.

Roasted Chickpeas

Ingredients:

- 1 can (15 oz) chickpeas, drained and rinsed
- 1 tablespoon olive oil
- 1/2 teaspoon smoked paprika
- 1/2 teaspoon garlic powder
- Salt to taste

Instructions:

1. Preheat the oven to 400°F (200°C) and line a baking sheet with parchment paper.
2. Toss chickpeas with olive oil, paprika, garlic powder, and salt.
3. Spread chickpeas on the baking sheet in a single layer.
4. Roast for 25-30 minutes, shaking the pan halfway through, until crispy. Serve warm or at room temperature.

Cucumber Bites with Cream Cheese

Ingredients:

- 2 large cucumbers, sliced into rounds
- 4 oz cream cheese, softened
- 2 tablespoons fresh dill, chopped
- 1 tablespoon lemon juice
- Salt and pepper to taste

Instructions:

1. In a bowl, mix cream cheese, dill, lemon juice, salt, and pepper.
2. Spread the cream cheese mixture on each cucumber slice.
3. Garnish with extra fresh dill if desired and serve immediately.

Caprese Salad Cups

Ingredients:

- 1 pint cherry tomatoes, halved
- 1/2 cup fresh mozzarella balls (bocconcini or ciliegine)
- Fresh basil leaves
- Balsamic glaze (optional)
- Salt and pepper to taste

Instructions:

1. Place halved cherry tomatoes, mozzarella balls, and fresh basil leaves in small serving cups.
2. Drizzle with balsamic glaze (optional) and sprinkle with salt and pepper.
3. Serve immediately.

Caramelized Onion Dip

Ingredients:

- 2 tablespoons olive oil
- 2 large onions, thinly sliced
- 1/2 teaspoon sugar
- 8 oz cream cheese, softened
- 1/2 cup sour cream
- 1/2 teaspoon garlic powder
- Salt and pepper to taste

Instructions:

1. Heat olive oil in a pan over medium heat. Add onions and sugar, cooking slowly, stirring occasionally, for 20-25 minutes until caramelized.
2. In a bowl, mix cream cheese, sour cream, garlic powder, salt, and pepper.
3. Stir in caramelized onions and mix well. Serve with chips or veggies.

Coconut Shrimp

Ingredients:

- 12 large shrimp, peeled and deveined
- 1/2 cup flour
- 1 egg, beaten
- 1 cup shredded coconut
- 1/2 cup breadcrumbs
- Salt and pepper to taste
- Vegetable oil for frying

Instructions:

1. Preheat oil in a frying pan over medium heat.
2. Dredge shrimp in flour, dip in beaten egg, and coat in a mixture of shredded coconut and breadcrumbs.
3. Fry shrimp in batches for 2-3 minutes per side until golden brown and crispy.
4. Drain on paper towels and serve with dipping sauce.

Veggie Fritters

Ingredients:

- 1 cup zucchini, grated and excess moisture squeezed out
- 1/2 cup carrot, grated
- 1/4 cup onion, finely chopped
- 1/2 cup all-purpose flour
- 1 egg, beaten
- 1/4 teaspoon garlic powder
- Salt and pepper to taste
- Olive oil for frying

Instructions:

1. In a bowl, combine grated zucchini, carrot, onion, flour, egg, garlic powder, salt, and pepper.
2. Heat olive oil in a pan over medium heat.
3. Scoop spoonfuls of the veggie mixture into the pan and flatten with a spatula.
4. Cook for 3-4 minutes per side until golden brown. Drain on paper towels and serve.

Taco Dip

Ingredients:

- 1 package cream cheese, softened
- 1/2 cup sour cream
- 1 packet taco seasoning
- 1/2 cup salsa
- 1 cup shredded cheddar cheese
- 1/2 cup black olives, chopped
- 1/4 cup green onions, chopped
- Tortilla chips for serving

Instructions:

1. In a bowl, mix cream cheese, sour cream, and taco seasoning until smooth.
2. Spread the mixture in a shallow dish.
3. Top with salsa, cheddar cheese, olives, and green onions.
4. Serve with tortilla chips.

Chicken Sliders

Ingredients:

- 1 lb ground chicken
- 1/4 cup breadcrumbs
- 1 egg
- 1 tablespoon Dijon mustard
- 1 teaspoon garlic powder
- Salt and pepper to taste
- 8 mini slider buns
- 1/4 cup mayonnaise
- Lettuce and tomato slices (optional)

Instructions:

1. Preheat the grill or a skillet over medium heat. In a bowl, combine ground chicken, breadcrumbs, egg, Dijon mustard, garlic powder, salt, and pepper.
2. Form the mixture into small patties and cook on the grill or skillet for 5-6 minutes per side until fully cooked.
3. Toast the slider buns and spread mayonnaise on the bottom of each bun.
4. Assemble the sliders with the chicken patty, lettuce, tomato, and top with the other bun. Serve immediately.

Roasted Garlic and Parmesan Popcorn

Ingredients:

- 1/2 cup popcorn kernels (or 1 bag microwave popcorn)
- 1/4 cup butter, melted
- 2 tablespoons grated Parmesan cheese
- 1/2 teaspoon garlic powder
- Salt to taste

Instructions:

1. Pop the popcorn according to package instructions or on the stovetop.
2. In a small bowl, combine melted butter, Parmesan cheese, garlic powder, and salt.
3. Drizzle the butter mixture over the popcorn and toss to coat evenly.
4. Serve immediately as a savory snack.

Fruit and Cheese Skewers

Ingredients:

- 1 cup grapes (red or green)
- 1 block cheddar cheese, cut into cubes
- 1 block mozzarella cheese, cut into cubes
- 1 cup strawberries, hulled
- Wooden skewers

Instructions:

1. Thread a grape, a cube of cheddar cheese, a cube of mozzarella, and a strawberry onto each skewer.
2. Arrange the skewers on a serving platter.
3. Serve immediately as a refreshing snack or appetizer.

Nacho Bites

Ingredients:

- 1 bag tortilla chips
- 1 cup shredded cheddar cheese
- 1 cup shredded mozzarella cheese
- 1/4 cup jalapeños, sliced
- 1/4 cup black olives, sliced
- Salsa and sour cream for serving

Instructions:

1. Preheat the oven to 375°F (190°C). Arrange tortilla chips on a baking sheet.
2. Top each chip with a small amount of cheddar and mozzarella cheese, sliced jalapeños, and black olives.
3. Bake for 5-7 minutes until the cheese is melted.
4. Serve with salsa and sour cream for dipping.

Parmesan and Herb Crackers

Ingredients:

- 1 cup all-purpose flour
- 1/2 cup grated Parmesan cheese
- 1/2 teaspoon dried rosemary
- 1/2 teaspoon garlic powder
- 1/4 teaspoon salt
- 1/4 teaspoon black pepper
- 1/4 cup cold butter, cubed
- 2-3 tablespoons water

Instructions:

1. Preheat the oven to 375°F (190°C). In a bowl, mix flour, Parmesan cheese, rosemary, garlic powder, salt, and pepper.
2. Cut in the cold butter until the mixture resembles coarse crumbs.
3. Add water, 1 tablespoon at a time, to form a dough.
4. Roll out the dough on a floured surface and cut into small cracker shapes.
5. Place the crackers on a baking sheet and bake for 10-12 minutes until golden. Let cool and serve.

Stuffed Mini Croissants

Ingredients:

- 1 package mini croissants (store-bought or homemade dough)
- 1/2 cup cooked chicken, shredded
- 1/4 cup cream cheese
- 1 tablespoon Dijon mustard
- 1/4 cup shredded cheddar cheese

Instructions:

1. Preheat the oven to 375°F (190°C). Unroll the mini croissant dough and separate into triangles.
2. In a bowl, mix shredded chicken, cream cheese, Dijon mustard, and cheddar cheese.
3. Place a spoonful of the mixture at the wide end of each croissant triangle and roll up tightly.
4. Place the stuffed croissants on a baking sheet and bake for 10-12 minutes until golden and crispy.
5. Serve warm.

Sweet and Savory Chex Mix

Ingredients:

- 3 cups Rice Chex cereal
- 3 cups Corn Chex cereal
- 1 cup pretzels
- 1 cup mixed nuts
- 1/2 cup butter, melted
- 1/4 cup honey
- 1/4 teaspoon cinnamon
- 1/4 teaspoon salt

Instructions:

1. Preheat the oven to 350°F (175°C). In a large bowl, combine the Chex cereals, pretzels, and mixed nuts.
2. In a separate bowl, mix melted butter, honey, cinnamon, and salt.
3. Pour the butter mixture over the cereal mixture and toss to coat evenly.
4. Spread the mixture on a baking sheet and bake for 10-15 minutes, stirring halfway through.
5. Let cool before serving.

Meat and Cheese Sliders

Ingredients:

- 8 mini slider buns
- 8 slices deli meat (turkey, ham, or roast beef)
- 8 slices cheese (Swiss, cheddar, or provolone)
- 1/4 cup mayonnaise
- 1 tablespoon mustard
- Pickles (optional)

Instructions:

1. Preheat the oven to 350°F (175°C). Slice the slider buns in half and place them on a baking sheet.
2. Spread mayonnaise and mustard on the bottom half of each bun.
3. Layer deli meat and cheese on each bun, then top with the other half of the buns.
4. Bake for 8-10 minutes until the cheese is melted and the buns are toasted.
5. Serve with pickles, if desired.

www.ingramcontent.com/pod-product-compliance
Lightning Source LLC
LaVergne TN
LVHW081343060526
838201LV00055B/2814